ENTER

ALSO BY JIM MOORE

The New Body
What the Bird Sees
How We Missed Belgium (with Deborah Keenan)
Minnesota Writes: Poetry (coeditor)
The Freedom of History
The Long Experience of Love
Writing with Tagore: Homages and Variations
Lightning at Dinner
What It's Like Here
Invisible Strings
Underground: New and Selected Poems
Prognosis

ENTER

POEMS

JIM MOORE

Graywolf Press

Published by Graywolf Press
212 Third Avenue North, Suite 485
Minneapolis, Minnesota 55401

www.graywolfpress.org

Published in the United States of America

ISBN 978-1-64445-339-1 (paperback)
ISBN 978-1-64445-340-7 (ebook)

2 4 6 8 9 7 5 3 1
First Graywolf Printing, 2025

Library of Congress Cataloging-in-Publication Data

Names: Moore, James, 1943– author.
Title: Enter : poems / Jim Moore.
Description: Minneapolis, Minnesota : Graywolf Press, 2025.
Identifiers: LCCN 2024045534 (print) | LCCN 2024045535 (ebook) |
    ISBN 9781644453391 (paperback) | ISBN 9781644453407 (epub)
Subjects: LCGFT: Poetry.
Classification: LCC PS3563.O618 E58 2025 (print) | LCC PS3563.O618
    (ebook) | DDC 811/.54—dc23/eng/20241001
LC record available at https://lccn.loc.gov/2024045534
LC ebook record available at https://lccn.loc.gov/2024045535

Cover design: Claire Zhang

Cover photo: JoAnn Verburg, *Enter*, 2024

For JoAnn, my sister Madeline, and Deborah Keenan.

CONTENTS

ENTER

PRELUDE

Life is short. Why not combine everything

into one poem: my seashell

from thirty years ago,

the little plastic cardinal

you gave me on our first pandemic Christmas,

the postcard propped on the windowsill. It's a Duccio of Mary

holding her baby close.

The baby has grabbed her veil with one hand,

her shoulder with the other. Everyone

everywhere is just holding on.

MORNING SONG

It's a lucky day for me
if they are burning on the hill,
the cut and fallen branches.
Fire consumes wood, smoke
consumes air. Lucky day
to see what burns and smokes
inside me. If I sit at the window
long enough, the moon
will come back. Is that enough then?
I don't mean is the moon enough,
but is the waiting for the moon?
I'm asking is the blue enough in Mary's robe
as she cradles her dead son in her lap.
It is Bellini's blue in the Accademia.
I stood for so long in front of it
that the guard, sitting on his little stool,
stopped whistling "Bridge
over Troubled Water" and stared at me
in silence. But I stayed right where I was.
I had fallen in love with her,
that feeling of being nowhere
and everywhere at once, the way
the gods felt
when there were still gods. Meanwhile,
it's 6 a.m. and there is smoky light
on the mountain, the hill, the olive trees,
those two birds hiding under the neighbor's red tiles.
Serve us, they sing, *us and us alone.*
Are they swallows or swifts?
After all these years I still don't know.

NO MORE PADDLING TONIGHT!

A beached kayak sits under a streetlight.
No more paddling tonight! Say *manatee*
and dream. Since an ode always sleeps inside
an elegy, the paddle shines in the light, its dark wood
still wet from the day that once was.

WHEN WE WERE ETERNAL

A man too old to be carrying a skateboard
is carrying a skateboard,
cradling it like a broken wing
as he walks down the middle
of the street, empty of traffic,
but filled with November sunlight
and November's long shadows.

Then the man is gone.
The true silence begins,
the one with two neon signs
at the entrance to the parking garage.
One says *ENTER* and one *EXIT.*
"More than enough of us have died,"
Tsvetaeva wrote during her plague year.
"Too long we've been howling like orphans."

Maybe that man was an angel
whose wing had fallen off.
Maybe he will have to cradle a skateboard
wherever he goes for the rest of his life.

"Concede forgiveness," she wrote.
Something inside us remembers
what it is like to be eternal. Is it
good luck or bad that we carry
that memory with us for as long as we live?

MOTHER

For JoAnn

My friend and I had a cat we called Mother.
I took the couch, my friend got the one bedroom
because he often had sex and needed
that private darkness. I had not yet had sex
of my own volition. No one knew
I had been raped. I was so unknowing
I barely knew it myself, how lost I was
to myself. I was maybe twenty. We loved that cat
that had wandered into our lives, rubbing our legs,
needing love and milk and a safe place
to sleep like any creature arriving on this earth
from God knows where and God knows why.
One hot August day I was sitting outside
when Mother joined me and sat on my lap,
a thing she had never done before.
And that was where she died. I called Jeff
who had gone to a motel somewhere
with his girl of the moment. "Mother died,"
I said. There was a long silence, then
he whispered quietly, "Oh, no,"
as if he wanted to keep his sorrow to himself.
Many years later I told my actual mother
about the rape. She cried a little and was angry
on my behalf. I was calm. Relieved.
Then life went on, as it does,
without much of a pause. I was not healed
by telling her, I am sorry to say.
I am still not at seventy-nine. The beautiful gray sky
of a rainy May day, and the lindens

coming into flower. That smell!
You and I both love it. (Did you know
all along I was writing this poem to you?)
Often at night we walk to the river
and stare down into the black current
which has reached flood stage
and sweeps everything before it.

THE POEM GOES ON

After Jennifer Grotz's "Edinburgh Meditation"

I thought I'd write a poem,
then thought better of it and read one instead:
a painting, horses, a moor, her sadness.
Then came a bridge, castles even, also bare branches
which in poems often mean
that the poet is seeing the world as beauty
stripped of all excess. Whatever comes next
life will not be as it was.

The poem goes on. The sun lowers,
as it so often does in poems. Somehow
being lost is at the heart of things: loneliness
understood as that most peculiar
of pleasures. The poem is very long.
On and on it goes, all of it
a sadness unraveling
into joy, and then, finally,
it ends and she is left with its echo:
how she wanted something beyond words.

In the course of reading her poem
I sometimes looked up and away from the page.
I saw the rise and dip, the stalled drift
of an eagle. I saw the snowy hill,
the river covered in ice. A woman in a mask
walked toward the hospital. Above her
an oak tree's branches reached up like a note to God,
still unsent. I saw another woman
clutching a pink phone as if it were a raft:
without it, who knows how long she would stay afloat.

Across the street, a broken balcony. Standing on it,
a man looked down and smiled at something only he could see.
I imagined he had a goldfish in a bowl.
I imagined he fed it every day,
swapping out cloudy water for clear.
It wasn't castles or a horse in Scotland.
It was what I had and it was everything.

FLY, PELICAN, FLY

What's this all about?
Let's do a list. Die
is last. Dawn is first. The sea says
the sea is all there really is. Fly,

pelican, fly. It's not enough to love. Not even
to die. May we somehow learn to live
with what sinks us. Here's what works in the end: Spain,
maybe. Flamenco. Friends at our side. Lorca, still alive.

THE ENTOMBMENT OF CHRIST

Caravaggio

He is almost too heavy to lift,
but still must be carried to the burial site.
He has a mother. She peers down at him
as if she has lost something
and is looking hard for it as she stares
into his pale face. The background
is black. It must be night. No one knows
the best way to carry him.
Death is so awkward.
A young man cries out. His trembling mouth
is wide open, his delicate wrist
as naked as flesh can be
when it needs someone to touch it.
Then there is that creature in the corner (it could be
any of us) who peers down
on the scene, trying to make out
how faraway life has no choice
but to carry us from life.

FIELD GOAL, MOONLIGHT, MEN WALKING TO WORK

Last night our team won in the final three seconds.
We beat our archrivals.
This morning at 6:10 a.m. the moon rides high
over the parking garage. Clearly
this isn't a poem at all. It is just a title:
FIELD GOAL, MOONLIGHT, MEN WALKING TO WORK.
I live in this world and no other. It is sad
how people in my country huddle together in a stadium
for comfort. But also beautiful in the way what's necessary
is also beautiful. It is late November, a little light
beginning to gather in my sky.
I love my darkness and my greed
for light. I often regret
not having had a calm and loving childhood.
Though in that life I might not have needed the moon
the way I do now. Who then would have written the poem,
FIELD GOAL, MOONLIGHT, MEN WALKING TO WORK?

IN THIS TOWN

Spoleto

In this town, mourning doves and roses, even in November.
In this town, silence more often than not.
In this town, old is where everyone is heading.
In this town, ten earthquakes in a single night:
we sleep in our clothes because who knows?
In this town, whoever knows?
In this town, all the streets climb slowly up.
If you are coasting sweetly down, you are not anymore
in this town. And in this town, an aqueduct
that carries water inside its stone body.
In this town, people will stand on the aqueduct,
then jump to their deaths holding hands.
In this town, whether or not you jump,
you don't know why you were born or why
some mornings the mourning dove sings
and some mornings it decides the world
doesn't deserve a song. In this town,
we ascribe motives to mourning doves
that don't sing. In this town, many believe in God
and are led by a light not known to us all.
In this town, the Senegalese man selling beads
stops at midday and holds his face up to the sun.
And even our neighbor in this town,
who won't be getting up again, smiles because you brought him
babah rum, and he loves babah. Always has and always will.

WHAT HELPS

It helps to be near time, but not right in the middle.
Helps to have the two dead parents to remind him

the floor drops out, and then you are stars, a moon,
all darkness all the time. Helps to remember pain

has a beginning, middle, and end.
When the back hurts more than the groin,

and the groin more than the blurred eye,
then he knows what it means

to be human. The human condition is not just about pain,
but when pain comes, step off to one side and take it

with you. Get out of the way of those others who don't
yet know who they really are and the cost of it all.

Let them be pretty and young or old and trying for dignity.
In other words, let them be. It helps to see her fierceness,

that woman with a plastic bag bent over double,
two canes, looking for wild asparagus,

crushing poppies underfoot.

NOTHING MORE

Today I have decided it is enough
having been born. Today, nothing more.
Except for the man in the blue jacket
lugging the suitcase in and out
of the parking garage as if he can't
make up his mind about whether or not
he has a car. The man with the suitcase
may not yet clearly understand
there is no escape from himself, whether or not
he drives away. He came into my life
as a stranger carrying a bag with nothing in it
that will save him. A nurse who works in the clinic below
is walking quickly, late to work. It is always late:
there is no way to catch up. No one knows for sure
what comes next, but no one needs to know.
How strange that the subject of life is death.

EVERYTHING IS NOT ENOUGH

Rereading Tsvetaeva.
She lived through her own plague years.
Did not actually live through them.
Hanged herself. Her desperation.
And yet she wrote
"moonlight through the attic window—
that's how far our banquet reaches!"
Her passion was what she had,
and yet, it was not enough.
When the dictator comes, he will be freely elected.
I will still walk
with my friend each Friday
along the abandoned railroad tracks.
Sometimes we will even laugh.
Tsvetaeva is writing about November.
Rain falls. Fog.
"Love's cross is heavy. We won't try to lift it."

HOW TO COME OUT OF LOCKDOWN

1

Someone will need to forgive me for being
who I am, for sneaking back to my blue chair

by the window where for the last three hundred seventy days
I have learned that to be alone is what is good for me. I pretend

to really belong with those who want to return to this world
with open arms, even though it has done to us

what it has done. I wish I could love like that
instead of wanting to turn my back on it all,

as if life in the world were a marriage
assumed too young and necessarily left behind.

Try as I might, I will never become
one of the world's faithful ones.

My naked face and your naked face,
maskless. A cold March dawn,

harsh sunlight, impersonal and honest,
mindless like the light from a surgeon's lamp

worn on the forehead as you peer down
into the wound. Nothing in this new life

is asked of me except to remember how small I am.

2

Sometimes the world won't let itself
be sung. Can't become a poem. Sometimes

we are sane, but sanity alone is not enough.
Warm moonlight and wind. I am sitting here,

simply breathing because there is no other way
to be with those who no longer can.

I don't know what to say about it all,
but if you do, please show me how to be you.

In the last play I saw fourteen months ago,
before there were no more plays,

they made a sea of the stage. Songs were chanted
on its shore. Lives lived. People pretended to die

and a ship sailed into the night. A moon. One star.
Afterward, applause. Then began that long silence

which it is now time for me to admit I have loved
beyond any reason or defense. Who among us

has not seen that star to the left
of the lockdown moon, shining

as the ship sets sail?

AT THE POETRY READING LAST NIGHT

There were stars projected onto a white sheet.
There was a grandfather's suicide, and
I felt lonely, agitated, strangely guilty,
as if the poet were my granddaughter
and I had not served her well. Afterward,
there was a moon, the first
in several days. The smell of lilies
of the valley. I felt the old familiar anger.
Now that I can't see well at night
it is a little dangerous to be me.

I am, on my good nights, like a pine tree
underneath a moon breaking through clouds:
I shine thanks to a light not my own.
I have made up too much about myself
that is not of that light. That quiet poise.
Not of that beauty. Maybe that is why
I am too often angry with the universe:
I try to outshine it. I am like a battlefield
after the war is over. Nothing is left
of the world as it once was. Trees
have been bombed into splinters.
The earth is broken. No one
wants to live there now.
There is a kind of monument you see
in such places. A plaque that gives the dates
of the battle and how many died.
I am like those monuments:
a reminder of the cost
of war.

I'm thinking of the poet
and her grandfather. Those galaxies
so far away. Unreachable. And yet, for that reason,
a comfort. I need to stand for something
beyond my own defeat. And that would be
what exactly? The word *humility*
comes to mind. If I make it
farther than that, I will let you know.

THE SMALL ONE

For Deborah and Corey

1

I've been a mess my whole life.
Why should that change now just because
I am seventy-nine?
I've tried forgiving my mother,
also myself. Five therapists. I've tried drinking
and not drinking. I've tried solitude,
living for months alone in a trailer
next to a fallow asparagus field.
Oceans are beautiful.
Mountains too.
But in both places I remained,
like the baby in my dream last night,
the small one, the one in need. Honestly,
helpless. Even here, today
among the olive trees and with someone I love nearby.

2

I can't seem to get it through my head
that we are born, then die, and anything in between
that isn't love is ridiculous.
I'm not going to change. I know that.
I remember that time my friend and I
were sitting in a pew in the back of a church.
I don't know why. A funeral? A wedding?
We were young and she had her last baby on her lap.
The baby smiled at me as if she knew

I would receive her. She lifted her arms
toward me. Her mother let me hold her.
In truth, this was a dream
that I had last night.

3

Today,
sitting here with these olive trees,
I remember that once upon a time
I was born and once upon a time
I will die. Once upon a time
I sat in sunlight under an olive tree
and while remembering a baby from a dream,
closed my eyes.

FINALLY STOPPED ASKING

Silver leaves, this cloudy sky, darkness
on the way. You aren't invited to be
as calm as they are. This full of a light that knows
it is passing and does not mind. You mind. You are close
to this world; but only so close, the same way
that a father is close to the daughter he is about
to walk down the aisle. Close,
but a thousand miles away. You hope
you will be kind to the darkness
which very soon will be taking you with it.
The word *stars* comes to mind, but they, too,
are not about you. Light-years away.

You no longer *have* a mother and don't yet
have a death. Last night, you finally
stopped asking. You feel sorry for anyone who thinks,
as you do, that happiness is an answer.
The empty stadium across the street
was lit up as if it was trying to be a party.

It matters that you saw
those two small turtles floating on a sunlit log
in Colorado on the long trip which somehow
you survived. And now, in the park,
a brass band with two trombones, a trumpet,
and the girl on the tuba giving it her all.
Sometimes what works is to sit on a bench
tapping your foot and clapping your hands
at the end along with everyone else.

VALENTINE'S DAY

Twenty below, again
and again, a man runs up the snowy hill
across the street.
Again and again, I don't.
But I am grateful, even so, for the epitaph
on that ancient Greek grave:
"Oh, so very sweet your touch . . .
I burn, I flower."

MY CALIFORNIA

In case you didn't know, birds-of-paradise don't always live and die
in pots. There is a world. Forest fires, earthquakes,
birds-of-paradise: I live here now, sunlight and shadow. It is sweet
to be seduced so easily: a little warm dirt
underfoot and suddenly I am smiling as if
I get the joke to which I am the punch line.
My father was born thirty miles from here, near
where the ocean begins, and he would swim
to uninhabited islands, where the problems
created by humankind don't feel
as if they have a point. Along came the Depression
and grandfather sold the orange grove.
My father dropped out of his community college,
hitchhiked to Decatur, Illinois, and that was that:
it turned out the world was flat, after all.
I grew up there, no bookstores, no birds-
of-paradise, no stone buddhas sitting quietly in gardens
next to cacti and persimmons, lavender, and permission
to be. That smile of my father's, a little sweet,
a little distant, a little too easy to misread
as peaceful. I don't have anyone
left on this earth
to disappoint the way
sons can disappoint fathers.
His things were hunting ducks and genealogy; my thing
is to disappear without leaving a trace.
There is no shame in that, I tell myself,
now that I am a temporary Californian.

MY VENICE

Sometimes the why of things

escapes me. I think my soul is like a fist
that on occasion opens. A man on the water bus yesterday

refused to wear a mask. Others yelled at him.
"Fuck you all!" he yelled back. A man two seats down

couldn't stand it a moment longer, put his hands
over his ears, buried his head in his crossed arms.

Meanwhile, the boat was surrounded on all sides
by open water. We don't get to live forever.

Suddenly it went dead quiet on the boat.
At that moment I was pretty much down on my knees.

An old man two rows up pulled out a newspaper
and pretended to be reading. I wanted to get off that boat

and find the nearest Bellini. Maybe the one in the Accademia
where the mother of God holds the child tightly

and looks down and away from us,
a sly look on her face, as if she knows the secret.

A tree to the left of her and one to the right.
Blue mountains and a sky rinsed clean

with a light not of this earth.

AFTER MICHAEL LONGLEY,
AFTER AMERGIN GLÚINGEL

I am the bat that vanishes
under the bridge in late September.
I am the little dancer in night air, drunk
on insects. See me over there by the couple drowning
in each other on the bench under the pine tree?
I am the velvet thing that whisks your ear lobes.
I am at home in a cave, a whisker in a dark hole.
I am encircled by rain, owned by wind.
I am a blossom if only you truly see me.
And autumn folds up my wings and carries me
to the underworld. The lightest death you'll ever know
is not your own. I am your shadow,
your melancholy, your eyes closed
against the world. I am your littlest mouse self
given wing. I squeeze through the keyhole
of your fear, you who remember the boy
who drowned twenty years ago: together
you worked for a month to build a raft.
It was summer, Lake Michigan. And there I was
under the green bench by the poison ivy, sitting
with the patience of a saint, wings folded,
waiting for the next darkness to come.

MEANWHILE

This morning, as if I knew no better, I walked out
into the world, hoping to be surprised.
My gray river was shining the way it does
when rain wants to fall, but can't quite.
Meanwhile, the work on the bridge goes on and on.
Unending brokenness. The red-winged blackbirds
keep insisting spring is here. They live in the river weeds
and don't know a thing about giving up. Near her end,
my mother called out to birds that weren't there.
"I do not understand why I must still be here," a man said,
one room down from my mother. His body
had been placed on a scale, as if being weighed
might make a difference. In her last days, my mother
mistook passing clouds for birds:
of all the mistakes I had known her to make,
that last one was the most beautiful, caught there
at the border of her life.
Those birds flew back into the clouds
as easily as life flies back into death.

IT'S NOT REST I NEED

I live near the place where ambulances leave for their emergencies. Sirens and sunrise. Streetlights and falling leaves. In defense of this planet, there was a pine tree I was able to stand next to after my mother's funeral. With the first light, pine trees come back. The clouds and the wind. It's not rest I need, but a deeper way to be the pine tree as it lists southward. And for the record, there is a small grove of ragged pine trees grazing in the sunlight, right now. *Grazing*, for they can be said to feed off the earth itself. Down the street someone brushes his hair, using a car window as a mirror: we do like the idea that we might fix ourselves. It is a fond and useless wish, falling needles, keeping us company on our slow ride down, we who will be grazed upon by the earth.

FEBRUARY

There are days called February. The word gray is given the keys to the city. Sometimes tenderness arrives out of nowhere, stays for a moment, and then is gone. Like a grown child who leaves home to make her way in the world. She goes away, she returns, then goes away again. You remain behind. She seems to understand you have no choice but to be who you are. Understands what it means to be February. She knows how lucky she is to have left home. To have left you behind. You know how lucky you are to have known her, even if only during one brief visit or another.

MINNEAPOLIS: 38TH AND CHICAGO

When the rain truly begins, people start running
as if rain is the problem. It is not rain. It is the soul
trying to stay afloat. The things soul does
include watching all eight seasons
of *Homeland*, following the breath; settling down again
each night into last light. The soul carries
too much weight, complains endlessly, and is,
as someone once said of it, unkindly,
a drama queen. At sixteen,
it's body was taken, and then left,
unclaimed, for decades. When the rain stops,
the sky has a pink moment
and the soul finds itself walking
on stolen land because history
is a long story of what has been stolen,
who stole it, and how they refuse
to give it back. After the pink moment
comes the true darkness.
At the corner of 38th and Chicago,
a sign reads "Nobody is illegal on stolen land."
Rush hour traffic. A small boy and his mother
wait to cross, hand in hand.

ETC.

Should I write that poem again,
the one about how hard it is to live
now that the end, etc.? The day
has been far too hot. A boy
was sitting by the water fountain,
his head in his hands, as if he was
playing hide-and-seek with himself,
hoping to be found. You and I
were in love, but as so often recently,
troubled about the great etc.
which even the moon can't charm away.
Still, it helps to be seen for who we really are:
the way you saw me last night
as we walked through the darkness
and you told me about the two bats
under the streetlight. I can't see that well
these days so you explained how maybe
they were fighting, maybe having sex.
You encircled me with your arm,
even though the night was etc.

BUT SHYLY

And words will come this birthday,
but shyly, like those swallows
that sleep under the bridges in Venice.
Once Gregory Corso and I
were together on my birthday in Venice.
We met by accident. He wrote a love poem to JoAnn.
Something about an angel. Who could blame him?
He was wilder than me. But I'd rather be the shy swallow,
wings folded, dozing in deep shadow
under that bridge near Antica Locanda Montin.
Each hour the loud bells reverberate
from the church by my bridge.
I count hours. I find words.
I write of love.

THE NEED IS SO GREAT

Sometimes I sit like this at the window and watch
the darkness come. If I'm smart, I'll put on Bach.

How far it always seems there is to go!
Maybe it is too easy that I speak so often

of late last light on a December day,
of that stubborn grass that somehow still remains green

behind the broken chain-link fence on the corner.
But my need is so great for the way light looks

as it takes its leave of us. We say
what we can to each other of these things,

we who are such thieves, stealing first
one breath and then the next. Bach, keep going

just this slowly, show me the way to believe
that what matters in this world has already happened

and will go on happening forever.
Light falling on the last

of the stricken leaves of the copper beech
at the end of the block is something to behold.

[handwritten annotation in right margin:] like a surgeon pulling it close to illuminate a friable vessel resistant to the suture & the blood obscuring the field of vision, the patient etherized on the table and who won't wake is among the living

NEVER TOO LATE

Never too late to return to Chinatown.
To walk Divison all the way to the park.
The old women do tai chi.
The middle-aged women practice
a circle dance with fans, long silks, and slippers.
Little kids go with the frantic running
between merry-go-round and mother.
Old men and young play ping-pong
with a vicious certitude that losing
and winning are as separate as death and life.
And the sycamores. Always the sycamores.

The women who wear city uniforms
dig in the dirt, doing something
necessary all around
the roots. Never too late to return.
That green bench is still there.
And the woman sitting on one end of it,
me on the other. Never too late to remember
how to look away from someone living
in her own world two feet away.

The deep tiredness is still an hour or two off
and then comes that room in the little hotel
where two bridges meet, the sound
of their traffic unceasing. Even at night
the dark sycamores shine. No, never
too late: and now, at last, it is time.

A CLEAR VIEW

1

I should love the world
more than I do. After all,
it made room for me eighty years ago
when the whole family was still alive
and we walked home from Al and Pauline's
in the newly fallen snow:
I fell a little behind everyone I loved,
as I've always liked to do.
How could I have known then
that the world is only the world
and there is not enough mercy
to go around? Still,
I would like to have risen more fully
to the occasion of my own birth.

2

        Two small boys, brothers,
hide in a corner of the café, their faces lit
with the light of life itself. They wait
to be found by their mother. There will be laughter.
She will hug one, then the other, then both
at once, and I will be there to see it.

A woman walks by with a key
dangling from a strap on her neck:
A key to a door I will never open.
I don't believe that death is either key or door.

I doubt it knows what it is at all.
Even so, when the time comes
I will bow down to it. Probably
I have gone on too long, not just
in this poem, but in life.
It seems I am late for everything.

3

I don't mind
not understanding the two people, a table away,
speaking German. Still, when they go
it's a relief. Silence again, and a clear view
of the oak across the street.

BONNARD

The Almond Tree in Blossom should be everyone's last painting.
The patches of blue and green on the ground, little afterthoughts.
The shaking glory of the white petals.
Everyone's last painting should have a bit of sky poking through.
It should always be spring one final time.
Try to remember there will be a last time
to give back to the world everything
it has given you. Everyone should stand quietly
under their last almond tree. It is the end
of a spring day, shadows growing long,
blossoms gone dark.

THE POEM I ALWAYS WANTED TO WRITE TO YOU

You wanted me to write a poem on a certain subject.
But what was it?
Since I can't remember,
I will write, instead, a love poem.
There will be a river, red-winged blackbirds,
and the month of May, ready once again
to save us. Winter will be over.
We will walk through the poem
as if it is a park. Since it is May,
that lilac bush will be there, the one
behind which we hid when we first decided
to touch each other. Night will come
in the poem I wanted to write
to you. And as always you will point me
in the direction of a favorite constellation.
Whether or not I see it, I will say I do.
But you can believe me about one thing:
this was a poem I needed to write, filled
with a shapeless arrangement of stars,
and a lilac bush waiting impatiently for us
at the corner of Western and Summit.

HAIBUN

Wearing nothing but a T-shirt, she is taping the wind with her recording device. "Be quiet," she orders. He is happy to comply. Now the rain again. Late November darkness. He forgot to say "thank you" last night. So this morning he has to start all over again. It's the same exhaustion as always, the same sound of rain as it falls, scraping dry catalpa leaves. Same wind. Same Sunday bells. Snow on the mountain. Same women making their slow way to the cathedral. Same little park with the broken bench.

I wake often these long November nights,
wondering how it will feel, the last time
we are able to hold each other.

TO THOSE WHO HAVE GONE ON AHEAD

Remember what it was like to be us? Remember
seagulls and pigeons, endless wars, plastic
filling up one ocean, then the next?

How did you bear it? Being us?
How did you manage to stand on the bridge
and look down at the river in sunlight,
the two men fishing so calmly, as if
the world wasn't on a timer about to go off?

How did you manage to look at the woman
walking those two ancient dogs and not break out
into tears? Each morning around nine, a neighbor
patrols my four surrounding blocks

with a big bag and does nothing
but pick up trash from the day before.
And the friend of mine who smiled at me
when I said I was cold and gave me
her sweater to wear, though it was also
a cold world for her. Can you tell me,

you who have gone on ahead,
and who have seen what we have done
to the world which was once yours,
what I am meant to do
with such tenderness?

WHERE I LIVE NOW

Spoleto

Mostly, the people are old. Mostly,
they have lived through a war or two.
At least nine earthquakes.
Parents long dead, of course.
When my old people stop to smell a flower,
it's not the first. When they look down
at the uneven road, they slow but don't stop.

Twelve bells ring at noon from three churches,
all at once. ~~It is too much sometimes.~~
They go on, my old people.
They gave up long ago,
but they go on.
Swallows and bats, wild asparagus
when the season is right.

Every night the moon
as if never seen before, as naked
and shining as on the last night
before the plague began.
What is most beautiful is what ruins us
for anything else. The first forsythia in bloom.

ONE STREETLIGHT IS WORKING

He sees a crow, a seagull, the snow falling
onto the bare branches of the three elms.
Now that he can't hear much, the sound
of a yellow school bus's motor
is the same as a stunned soul
grinding up a hill:
he was never alone.

TO BE!

To be a willow tree! In sunlight!
And leaning over a white picket fence!
Far away from everything I understand of the world!
To be born!
Never to die!
To be that woman over there opening the wooden gate behind which
    she lives!
So blissfully to open a door!
So not me!
To be the willow!
To know right from wrong!
Sunlight from shadow!
Life from death!
To know so much and to forget it all!
To be forgotten when the new moon has barely set!
Darkness! Ancient! Everywhere! Unending!

ABOUT TO BE

For Maryka and LuLu and Aaron

I want to go back to the day
before I was born: the longest day of the year,
a beautiful June day in Decatur, Illinois.
A mother-to-be, a father-to-be, such happiness
in the prospect. As for me, I was swimming that day
in the ocean, though getting closer to shore.
Eyes closed, the tide coming and going, the way
air was a thing so far away I didn't need to give it
any thought at all. Afterward, life was as I should have
expected: happiness, sadness, confusion, shame, grief, joy.
All well and good, but to be swaddled again in the deep dark sea,
to be surrounded on all sides, buoyant. To be about to be!

HERE AND HERE AND HERE

For the darkness and the light, I am here.
For the anger and the fear.
For the *ENTER* in green and the *EXIT* in red.
That nurse walking to work
fifty years ago:
it is not quite dawn. She wears scrubs.
She is intent and on her way.
She will help as best she can.
We all, at least once in our lives,
will help as best we can. For the two working
streetlights and for the three too broken to bring light,
I am here. For the Greyhound bus, heading to Taos:
where I was coming from I no longer remember.
For *no longer remember*, I am more and more here.
And for shaking the two rugs at dawn.
I love to watch the dust fly.
For the crecent moon disrobing
into light: here. When I put the rug again
under your feet, you wiggle your toes
with such pleasure. Meanwhile,
the sun comes up. Very soon again, the darkness.
And I am here for this, too, because I was born
and the earth, too, was born,
and we are in it together, both of us here
for this day, third shortest of the year.
For the three spindly trees just planted,
bare as December: here and here and here.

LAST DAY

Say what you will, I stayed
as long as I could. I was often alone,
but not lonely. I was sad,
but not only.

The mountain barely visible in the distance.
The sound of the neighbor's voice, for once
not angry. The two bells
of 7:30 a.m. Now the woman,
two doors away, who coughs
is coughing again.

From now on in this life,
every day a last day. Suddenly,
it is August again. Heat
turns the sky purple,
a deep bruise. Even if it heals,
everything will feel more tender
than before and more helpless.

THE HAPPINESS ON THE OTHER SIDE OF HAPPINESS

Seward Park

Kids swing and old men sit. That's the way
we do it at the park. A division of tasks
right here where Division ends
and Canal begins. Sit in shade, if sitting
is your fate. Try not to be afraid,
even though you are not part
of this world, just visiting here
where two bridges cross a river.
Four teenagers, on the bench opposite,
are getting stoned. They laugh, and one says
"Fuck that." You do not, anymore,
get the joke. Sparrows and ravens take turns
in the sycamore. The boy's T-shirt says
City Loser. His face, sweet and nervous,
wanting so much to find something funny
which he might use for cover.
It was good being born, but this thing
about coming to the end is yet
another kind of happiness:
you will sit here long after they leave
until the day finally begins to close down
because after so much light,
darkness, too, is beautiful.
Meanwhile, the girls on the bench
are getting still more stoned. One says
"Oh, my God!" as she looks up into leaves:
light is a miracle she suddenly sees she
is a part of. But the other girl doesn't look up.

She continues playing with her hair
as if it is a complicated musical instrument
of her own making, which she has mastered
over many years of practice.

ENVOI

A woman lets down her hair
as she comes out of the parking garage
so her baby, riding on her mother's back,
can play with her hair. You, too, my book,
let down your hair. Be that kind of mother.

ACKNOWLEDGMENTS

With thanks to the following publications for publishing poems from this book, some of them in earlier versions and with different titles:

The Academy of American Poets' *Poem-a-Day*: "The Need Is So Great"

The Adroit Journal: "Bonnard" and "Where I Live Now"

The Brooklyn Rail: "The Poem Goes On," "Valentine's Day," "My California," "But Shyly," and "To Be!"

Catamaran: "Finally Stopped Asking"

The Ilanot Review: "Everything Is Not Enough"

Image Journal: *"The Entombment of Christ"* and "My Venice"

The Nation: "Fly, Pelican, Fly"

The New Yorker: "Morning Song," "Mother," and "How to Come Out of Lockdown"

The New York Review of Books: "After Michael Longly, After Amergin Glúingel"

Plant-Human Quarterly: "It's Not Rest I Need"

Plume: "Last Day" and "The Happiness on the Other Side of Happiness"

Poetry London: "Nothing More"

The Sun: "About to Be"

The Threepenny Review: *"Prelude"*

The Yale Review Online: "Field Goal, Moonlight, Men Walking to Work" and "Meanwhile"

"Mother" also appeared in the anthology *We've Got Some Things to Say*, edited by Mary Simmerling, published by Amherst Writers & Artists Press, 2024.

The Marina Tsvetaeva quotes in "When We Were Eternal" and "Everything Is Not Enough" are from Christopher Whyte's translation of *Moscow in the Plague Year: Poems*, published by Archipelago Books, 2014.

The older I get the more I realize that we are all in it together: I could not have made this book without the help of editors and friends along the way. Time and again I felt stuck. Time and again you came to the rescue.

Four people read various drafts of the book from beginning to end and gave invaluable feedback: thank you Carmen Giménez, Deborah Keenan, Gretchen Marquette, and JoAnn Verburg.

I have the great good fortune of having had Graywolf Press as my publisher since 2005. Carmen Giménez is not only the publisher of Graywolf, but she was also my editor for *Enter*. She read the book with care and with ferocious attention to details, large and small. It is a better book for this attention and this care. Deep thanks!

Many, many thanks to editors Jeff Shotts and Brittany Torres Rivera for their careful and rigorous work in helping usher *Enter* into the world.

And I want to thank everyone else at Graywolf who has worked so hard in support of the book. You have had my back for two decades and for five books. What amazing good fortune!

JIM MOORE is the author of eight books of poetry, including *Underground: New and Selected Poems, Invisible Strings,* and *Prognosis.* His poetry has appeared in the *Nation,* the *New Yorker,* the *New York Review of Books,* the *Paris Review,* and elsewhere. He has been writing poetry for almost six decades. A recipient of a Guggenheim Fellowship in Poetry, he lives in Minneapolis, Minnesota, and Spoleto, Italy, with his wife, the photographer JoAnn Verburg.

Graywolf Press publishes risk-taking, visionary writers who transform culture through literature. As a nonprofit organization, Graywolf relies on the generous support of its donors to bring books like this one into the world.

This publication is made possible, in part, by the voters of Minnesota through a Minnesota State Arts Board Operating Support grant, thanks to a legislative appropriation from the arts and cultural heritage fund. Significant support has also been provided by other generous contributions from foundations, corporations, and individuals. To these supporters we offer our heartfelt thanks.

To learn more about Graywolf's books
and authors or make a tax-deductible donation,
please visit www.graywolfpress.org.

The text of *Enter* is set in Haarlemmer MT Std.
Book design by Rachel Holscher.
Composition by Bookmobile Design & Digital
Publisher Services, Minneapolis, Minnesota.
Manufactured by Versa Press on acid-free,
30 percent postconsumer wastepaper.